Rap Your World

Rapping Rhymes about Sports

Thomas Kingsley Troupe

BLACK RABBIT BOOKS

Hi Jinx is published by Black Rabbit Books
P.O. Box 3263, Mankato, Minnesota, 56002.
www.blackrabbitbooks.com

Jen Besel, editor; Michael Sellner, designer;
Omay Ayres, photo researcher

Library of Congress Cataloging-in-Publication Data
Names: Troupe, Thomas Kingsley, author.
Title: Rapping rhymes about sports /
by Thomas Kingsley Troupe.
Description: Mankato, Minnesota : Black Rabbit
Books, [2021] | Series: Hi Jinx. Rap your world |
Includes bibliographical references. |
Audience: Ages: 8-12 years. |
Audience: Grades: 4-6. |
Identifiers: LCCN 2019031828 (print) |
ISBN 9781623103248 (Hardcover) |
ISBN 9781644664209 (Paperback) |
ISBN 9781623104184 (eBook) |
Subjects: LCSH: Sports—Juvenile literature. |
Rap (Music)—Juvenile literature.
Classification: LCC GV705.4 .T76 2021 (print) |
LCC GV705.4 (ebook) | DDC 796—dc23
LC record available at https://lccn.loc.gov/2019031828
LC ebook record available at https://lccn.loc.gov/2019031829

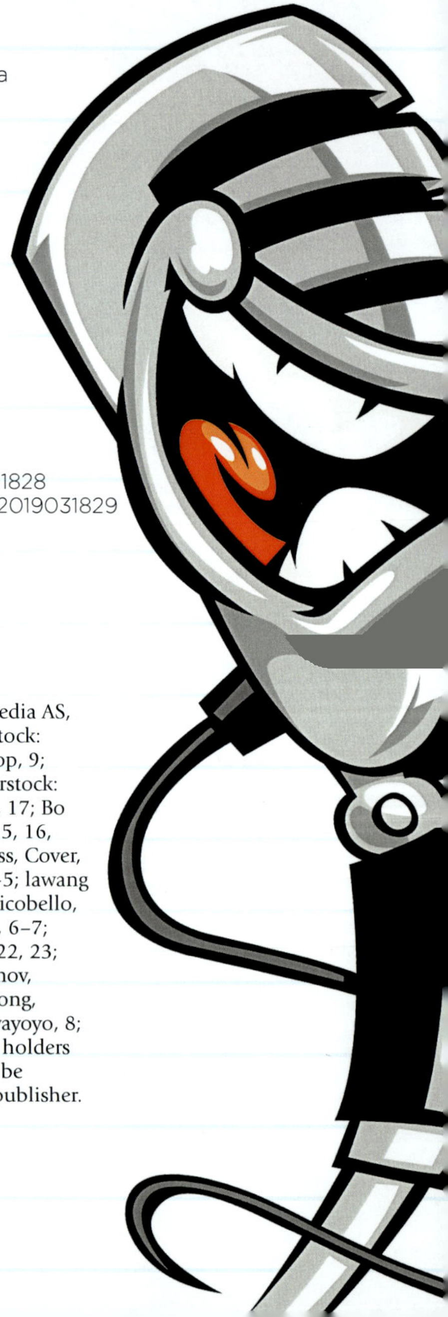

Image Credits
Alamy: BNP Design Studio, 19; Matthew Cole, 20; YAY Media AS, 6; Dreamstime: Dennis Crow, 11; Maciej Sojka, 14–15; iStock: Adelevin, 4, 6–7; artisticco, 17; Big_Ryan, 2–3; KeithBishop, 9; mike-artfx, 19; squirtgunn, 12–13; willierossin, 9; Shutterstock: ADudkov, 3, 21; Angeliki Vel, 19; Arcady, 1; Artisticco, 14, 17; Bo Secher, 12; Christopher Hall, Cover, 3, 4–5, 6, 8, 11, 12, 15, 16, 19; Christos Georghiou, 9; ChromaCo, 6–7, 8, 11; darikuss, Cover, 4–5; designer_an, 17; Gulman, 11; Kong Vector, Cover, 4–5; lawang design, 21; Memo Angeles, 1, 10–11, 20; Nosyrevy, 12; opicobello, 11; Pasko Maksim, 16, 23, 24; penang, Cover, 4–5; PILart, 6–7; pitju, 5, 9, 21; Ron Dale, 5, 8, 12, 16, 20; Ron Leishman, 22, 23; Rosovskyi, Cover, 4–5; Rvector, Cover, 4–5; Sergey Bogdanov, Cover, 14, 15; STREET STYLE, Cover, 1, 4; Tanawat_intawong, 14–15; totallypic, 14–15; Tueris, Cover, 1; Verzzh, 18; Yayayoyo, 8; your, 18; Every effort has been made to contact copyright holders for material reproduced in this book. Any omissions will be rectified in subsequent printings if notice is given to the publisher.

Contents

Chapter 1

Rap Your World!

Yo, listen up readers. Hear the words that I'm sayin.'

Get behind the **turntable**, and drop some beats that are slayin'.

Pairing rapping and sports is a game-winning notion,

It's sure to get your head and feet

ready for motion.

It's time to drop some **lyrics** about those things we call sports,
From the football fields to the basketball courts.
All the goals you can score with the soccer balls you kick,
There's a ton of sports to choose from, so please take your pick.

Yo, we'll rap about the sports you can play in the water,
All the games you can play if you're a son or a daughter.
You like extreme sports? Word, we'll cover those too.
So dive right in—there's so much to do!

Chapter 2
Outdoor Sports

Baseball is the sport known as America's pastime,
Pop flies, base hits, home runs **sublime**.
Using wooden bats, big gloves, and some cleats,
They're special shoes with spikes you use on your feets!

Grab your shoulder pads, and head out under the lights.

Need an extra point? Kick the ball through the uprights.

Touchdowns and first downs make the fans cheer and cackle.

Football is played many ways including touch and tackle.

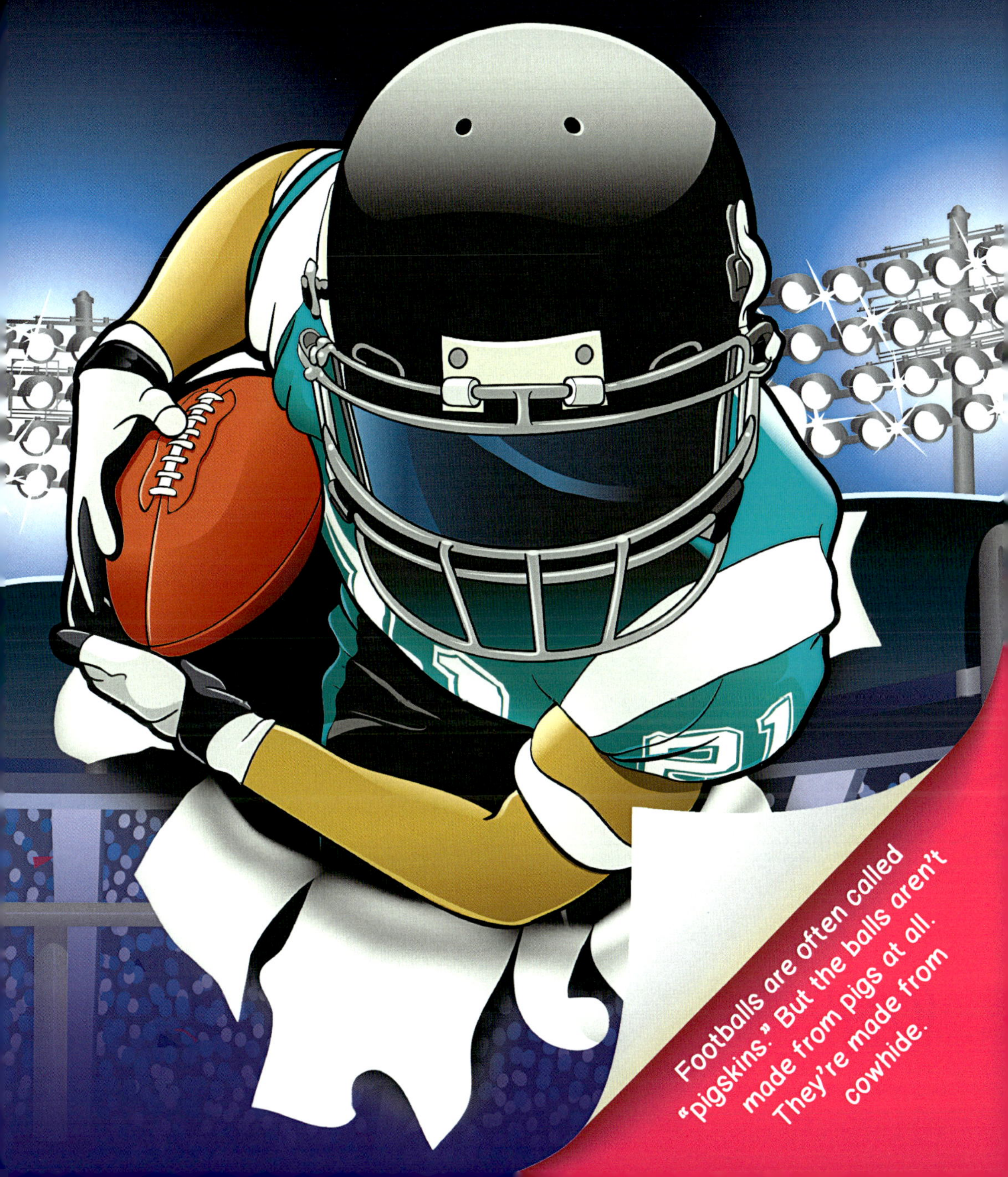

Footballs are often called "pigskins." But the balls aren't made from pigs at all. They're made from cowhide.

If we're talking popular sports, soccer's as big as it gets,
Players running around the field kicking balls into nets.
You can use your feet and head; but don't use your hands.
Yo, those cheers are straight up noisy from the fans in the stands!

American Indians created lacrosse hundreds of years ago.

Lacrosse is another sport that's played on a field.
Players wear a face mask, which works like a shield.
Tossing the ball back and forth using sticks with a net,
It's the fastest growing school sport. Have you tried it yet?

Chapter 3

Indoor Sports

A favorite indoor sport, and I'm telling you all,
Is the one where you dribble—I'm talking basketball!
Make a basket from the three-point line, the fans get loud.
Last-second winning points really excite the crowd!

The first basketball hoops were peach baskets.

Volleyball is played in a gym or out on a beach.

Jumping high to block the ball really depends on your reach.

The ball is served over the net to bump, **set**, and **spike**.

Diving to keep the ball inbounds is a move I really like.

Do you like to tumble or flip or do **acrobatics**?
Yo, then I'm pretty sure you're going to love gymnastics!
Swinging from rings, doing handstands on a beam,
Gymnasts kick it solo and sometimes on a team.

curling

Different kinds of sports? Yo, we're giving you a slice.

Curling's a funky sport that you play by sweeping ice!

You send a heavy stone toward the **house** and watch it slide.

Two teammates with brooms help it along, control its glide!

Chapter 4

In the Water and the Air

What's a sport for athletes who like to keep cool?
Swimming is the one because it's done in a pool.
Racing against others, all while staying in their lane,
Some events are 60 laps. Yo, that's kind of insane!

If you're looking for another sport to keep you afloat,
Then join up with a rowing crew where you paddle a boat.
Grab your oars and your teammates and get ready to race.
Rowing together as a group will keep you at a speedy pace!

The first recorded swim race was held in Japan more than 2,050 years ago!

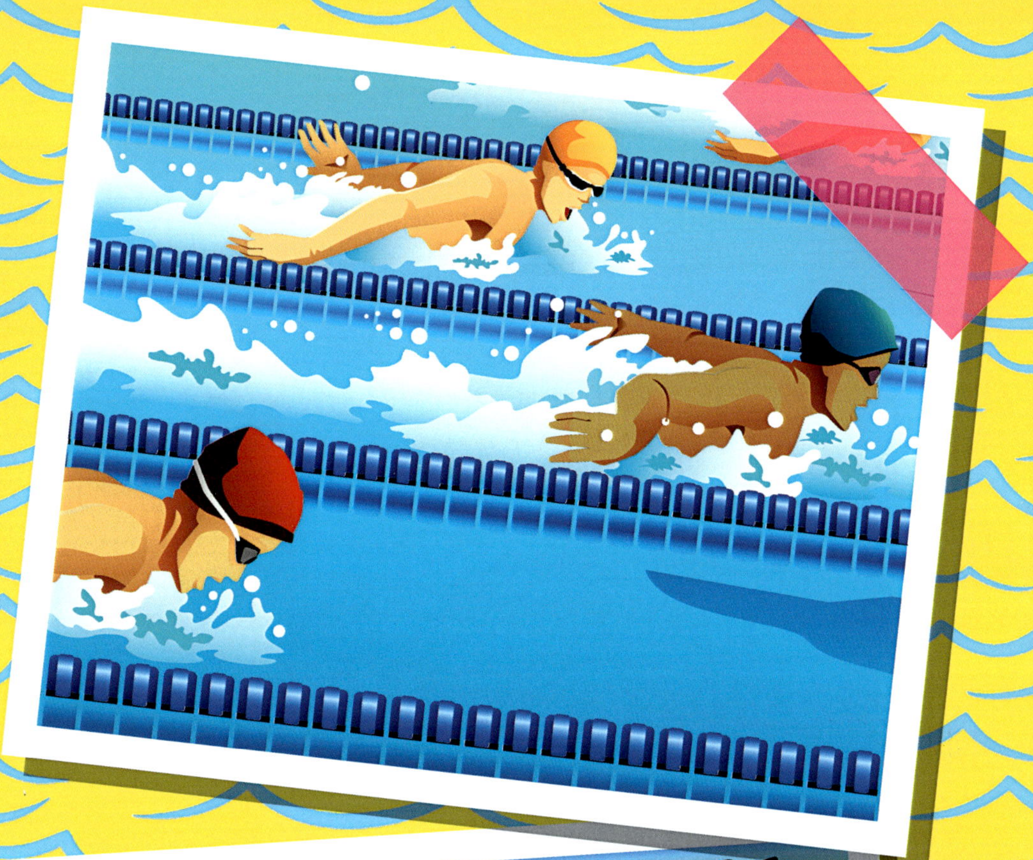

Put on your hat and gloves, and strap your feet to your board.
Slash the sky when you're airborne like a knight with a sword!
Snowboarding is a sport of speed and air time,
Big jumps, spins, and flips—the fun's almost a crime.

The first snowboard was called a "snurfer." The word combined "snow" with "surfer."

Motocross is a sport that an extreme athlete likes,
Racing other riders and hitting jumps on their bikes.
Rev the engine, hold on tight as they rip across dirt,
Wearing helmets and pads to be sure they're not hurt.

Chapter 5

Get in on the HiJinx

What's up, sport? Think you can write a rap about what it's like on the court? Of course, you can! First, dig up some information about the sports you like. Next, think of words about sports that are easy to rhyme. Maybe avoid badminton! Get the last words in each line to rhyme and give it a test. Practice and work on your rhymes until they're the best!

Take It One Step More

1. Did you read the lines to a beat? If you didn't, tap your hand on your leg in a steady rhythm. Try reading the words in time to the beat. How does that change your understanding of the information?

2. Rapping is a form of musical poetry. Is rapping a good way to learn information?

3. Have someone else read the raps out loud. Do they put **accents** in the same places you do?

GLOSSARY

accent (AK-sent)—an emphasis put on part of a word

acrobatics (ak-ruh-BAT-iks)—stunts like jumping, balancing, tumbling, and swinging from a bar

house (HOWS)—the rings or circles on the ice in curling toward which play is directed

lyric (LEER-ik)—the words of a song

rev (REV)—to cause an engine to run more quickly

set (SET)—a skill in volleyball in which a player directs the ball to a point where a player can spike it into the opponent's court

spike (SPIHK)—a type of attack in volleyball where the ball is hit down over the net with good force and speed

sublime (sub-LYM)—beautiful or impressive enough to create a feeling of admiration and wonder

turntable (TURHN-tay-buhl)—the part of a record player that turns the record

LEARN MORE

BOOKS

Braun, Eric. *Awesome, Disgusting, Unusual Facts about Sports.* Our Gross, Awesome World. Mankato, MN: Black Rabbit Books, 2019.

Pearson, Yvonne. *12 Great Tips on Writing Poetry.* Great Tips on Writing. Mankato, MN: 12-Story Library, 2017.

Weird But True! Sports: 300 Wacky Facts about Awesome Athletics. National Geographic Kids. Washington D.C.: National Geographic, 2016.

WEBSITES

Sports Facts for Kids
www.softschools.com/facts/sports/

Sports: Poems for Kids
poets.org/text/sports-poems-kids

Writing a Rap – Getting Started
www.youtube.com/watch?v=o6NZoTqWLq4

TIPS FOR WRITING YOUR RAPS

Having trouble finding the right word to rhyme? Try using a word that's close. If you rap fast enough, anyone listening might not even notice the words don't rhyme.

It helps to have a beat in mind when coming up with rhymes. Try counting out the beats in your head. Then when you start the next line, go for the same beat.

The best rappers know raps are never perfect the first time. They are always changing things. Every time you edit your rhymes, you're making them stronger.